# Fort Chipewyan Homecoming

# Fort Chipewyan Homecoming

WE ARE STILL HERE

NATIVE AMERICANS TODAY

## A Journey to Native Canada

by **Morningstar Mercredi**
Photographs by Darren McNally

L Lerner Publications Company ● Minneapolis

Series Editors: LeeAnne Engfer, Gordon Regguinti
Series Consultants: W. Roger Buffalohead, Juanita G. Corbine Espinosa

*Illustrations by Carly Bordeau*

*This book is available in two editions:*
Library binding by Lerner Publications Company
Soft cover by First Avenue Editions
241 First Avenue North
Minneapolis, MN 55401

ISBN: 0-8225-2659-X (lib. bdg.)
ISBN: 0-8225-9731-4 (pbk.)

LIBRARY OF CONGRESS CATALOGING-IN-PUBLICATION DATA

Mercredi, Morningstar.
    Fort Chipewyan homecoming : a journey to native Canada / by Morningstar
Mercredi ; photographs by Darren McNally
      p. cm.
    Includes bibliographical references.
    Summary: Twelve-year-old Matthew Dunn learns about the traditional ways of
his Chipewyan, Cree, and Métis ancestors on a trip to Fort Chipewyan, in Alberta,
Canada.
    ISBN 0-8225-2659-X (hardcover : alk. paper).  —  ISBN 0-8225-9731-4 (pbk. :
alk. paper)
    1. Chipewyan Indians—Social life and customs—Juvenile literature. 2. Métis—
Juvenile literature. 3. Cree Indians—Social life and customs—Juvenile literature.
4. Fort Chipewyan (Alta.)—Juvenile literature. [1. Chipewyan Indians—Social life
and customs. 2. Métis—Social life and customs. 3. Cree Indians—Social life and
customs. 4. Indians of North America—Canada—Social life and customs. 5. Fort
Chipewyan (Alta.)] I. McNally, Darren, ill. II. Title.
E99.C59M47   1997
971.23'2—dc20                                          96-15786

Manufactured in the United States of America
1 2 3 4 5 6 – JR – 02 01 00 99 98 97

*This book is dedicated with love to my nieces
and nephews: Scotty, Cory, Carmen, Sheri,
Lori-Lee, Nelson, Brandon, Jody, and Dream.
In loving memory of my late grandparents,
Jonas and Annie Piche and Emile Mercredi.
Special mention goes to all the grandmothers
of great Turtle Island, especially Josephine and
Isabelle Mercredi. Thank you for the memories,
Rita F. (Piche) and John L. Mercredi, I love you
both. Thank you, David Dunn, for sharing our
beautiful, strong son, Matthew Dunn (Bear Walker).*

## Preface

I grew up in Fort Chipewyan. I have so many fond memories of sitting by Lake Athabasca, listening to the cold northern wind howl beneath the moon, and of summer days when the hot sun stroked my hair, consoling me. I could take a short walk from the town of Fort Chipewyan and be in the bush, alone with my thoughts and at peace with nature. The land and Lake Athabasca have always been a source of strength and comfort to me.

The Native people of Fort Chipewyan have endured many changes as a result of European influences such as government, churches, and boarding schools. The people survived the changes and remain strong in our culture and our relationship to the land. This is evident in the respect most Native people have for the land, water, and animals.

Like many northern communities and reserves, Fort Chipewyan faces some challenges that are the legacy of oppression. But Fort Chipewyan is an isolated town, and while the world changes, Fort Chipewyan remains quiet and still. It seems to be in its own time zone.

I was so excited when summer arrived. I brought my son Matthew home to visit our relatives and to take in the beauty of Fort Chipewyan and Lake Athabasca.

Going home allows my heart and spirit to rest. Fort Chipewyan is a place where my people have lived for thousands of years, a place where I can breathe clean air and drink fresh water. My fondest childhood memories are of being raised with my late grandparents, Jonas and Annie Piche, in an area of town called Dog Head. There I played in fields of tall grass and ran around on rocky hills.

My grandpa used to lay spruce branches on the floor of our tent to use as a mattress. The smell of spruce trees takes me back to the safe place I knew as home. I recall the sound of my grandparents speaking in Chipewyan to each other and laughing. I miss hearing the loons sing and watching eagles soar in clear skies. On a clear night I would sit and watch the Northern lights dance with my ancestors. I used to imagine thousands of caribou hooves pounding the earth as they migrated across this great land. My heart remains with the earth, and my spirit waits to return home.

I hope you will enjoy this brief journey to our relations, the animals, the land, the waters, and the people of Fort Chipewyan.

—*Morningstar Mercredi*

*Morningstar Mercredi*

7

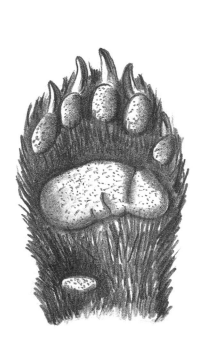

Matthew John Dunn is 12 years old. He lives in Canada, in Alberta part of the time and in Saskatchewan part of the time. Matthew's Indian name is *Sus Nakáhdul,* which means Bear Walker. He received his Indian name in a naming ceremony when he was ten years old. But most of the time people just call him Matthew.

Matthew has an interesting mixed heritage. His father, David, is English, Scottish, and Irish Canadian. His mother, Morningstar, is Métis, Denedeh (Chipewyan), and Cree Indian, as well as Scottish. *Métis* is a French word that means "mixed." The term goes back to the time when Europeans first came to North America, and some Europeans married Indian people. People whose parents were French and Indian were called Métis. The word *Denedeh* means "the people" in the Chipewyan language.

Matthew's parents were divorced when he was three years old. Since then, Matthew spends alternate years with each parent—one year with his mother, the next year with his father, and so on. His dad lives in Watrous, Saskatchewan. His mom lives in Edmonton, Alberta. Both cities are home for Matthew.

It isn't easy for him to go back and forth between his parents. When he is with one, he misses the other. And the parent he is away from misses him. He also has to change schools every year, so he often loses contact with his friends. On the positive side, he does get to travel a lot. Everywhere he goes, he meets new people.

This year Matthew and his mother are going to spend a week in Fort Chipewyan, where Morningstar grew up. Fort Chipewyan is a small, isolated community in northeastern Alberta on the edge of Lake Athabasca. This vacation will be a chance to visit relatives and friends and a time for Matthew to learn more about his mom's heritage. They will be there for a celebration called Treaty Days.

*Matthew's parents are divorced, but he spends a lot of time with each of them. Both parents attend Matthew's important track meets and other sports events.*

Fort Chipewyan is the oldest European settlement in Alberta. It was built in 1788. The fort became the headquarters for the fur trade in western Canada. Many Native people, including the Crees and the Chipewyans, trapped and hunted animals and traded the furs to English and French traders. The Indians stayed at Fort Chipewyan and other forts during the trading season, returning to their homes to hunt, fish, and trap.

Opposite: *Fort Chipewyan is in the northeastern corner of Alberta, at the edge of Lake Athabasca. The town* (top left) *bears little resemblance to the old fort* (below left), *which was built in 1788 and torn down in the 1930s.*

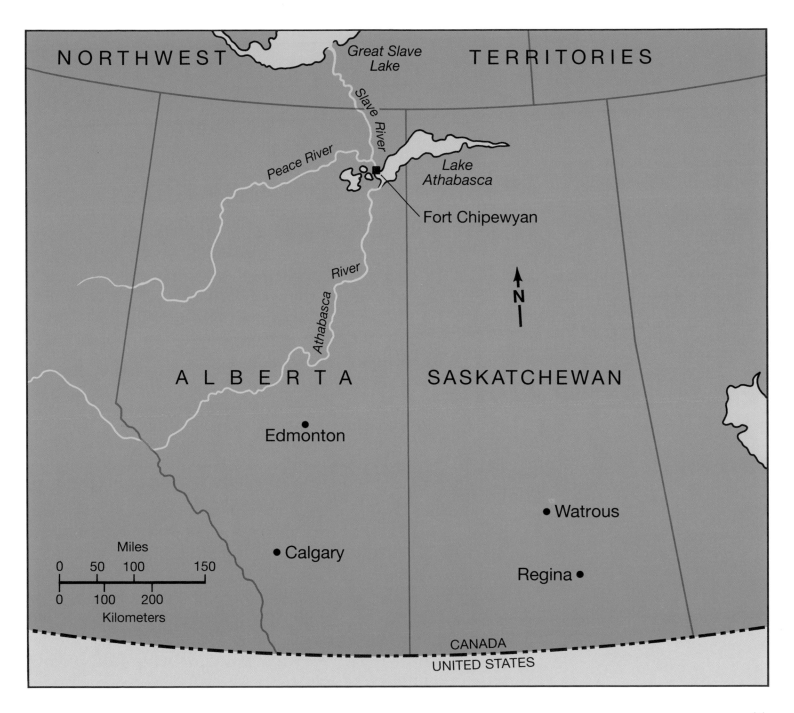

NORTHWEST                    TERRITORIES

Great Slave
Lake

Slave River

Peace River

Lake
Athabasca

Fort Chipewyan

N

Athabasca River

ALBERTA                SASKATCHEWAN

• Edmonton

• Watrous

Miles

0    50    100    150

• Calgary

Regina •

0    100    200

Kilometers

CANADA

UNITED STATES

Both the Crees and the Chipewyans have lived in Canada for thousands of years. The Crees lived in the forests of eastern and northern Canada, and on the plains of central Canada. The Chipewyans occupied a large territory in northwestern Canada, in the subarctic regions. The Chipewyans near Lake Athabasca once had a very large population. In 1792, however, nearly 90 percent of the Chipewyans died, of diseases brought by European settlers and of starvation.

Traditionally, the original peoples of Canada lived off the land. They hunted and fished. They picked plants and berries to eat and to use as medicine. The Chipewyans depended mostly on caribou for their survival. They ate caribou meat and made clothing and teepees from caribou skin.

In the modern world, many Indian people live in cities, as Matthew and his mother do. They buy their clothes and food at stores. Still, most Native people try to maintain ties to traditional culture in a variety of ways, such as speaking the language, dancing, and doing traditional crafts like beadwork. In Fort Chipewyan, some people live close to the land, as their ancestors did. They hunt and fish.

It had been four years since Matthew was in Fort Chipewyan. The last time he was there, he visited his late great-grandfather, Jonas Piche. Matthew knew Fort Chipewyan wouldn't be the same without his great-grandfather. Matthew remembered Jonas well. He had always teased Matthew and made him laugh.

Finally the day arrived for Matthew and his mother to fly on a small plane to Fort Chipewyan. The 45-minute flight from Edmonton to Fort Chipewyan was fun. Matthew could see trees, lakes, and rivers stretching out below for miles and miles.

There is no year-round road leading to Fort Chipewyan. Because the town is surrounded by water and wetlands, building a road would be difficult and expensive. During the summer, people fly in or travel by boat along the Athabasca River to Lake Athabasca, then to Fort Chipewyan. In the winter, people can drive over the frozen rivers, bogs, and lake.

When Matthew and his mother arrived in Fort Chipewyan, they settled in at one of their relatives' houses. Then they went for a walk to Monument Hill, overlooking the lake. Water splashed against the rocks at the bottom of the hill, and the breeze smelled fresh. Matthew noticed how quiet it was compared to rush-hour traffic in Edmonton.

The moon rose. Dogs barked, and mosquitoes buzzed around Matthew and Morningstar's heads. Matthew remembered Monument Hill from the last time he had been there. Now the hill seemed smaller to him. From where they stood, he could see the historical museum—that was one of the first places he wanted to go the next day. They walked home in the cool evening, tired from traveling all day.

*Matthew looks at a model of the old Fort Chipewyan, the fur trading headquarters of northwestern Canada.*

*T*he next morning after breakfast, Matthew and his mom got ready to go visiting and sightseeing.

First they went to the museum, where they saw a model of the old Fort Chipewyan. The fort no longer exists—it was destroyed in the 1930s. Fort Chipewyan is now just a small town. Matthew thought it would be interesting to go back to the days when Fort Chipewyan was a trading post, but he would miss living in the modern world.

From the museum, they went to visit a Métis elder named Maria Houle. She showed them the beadwork she did on moccasins and jackets. The beadwork was very detailed and beautiful, with many colors.

"It must take you a long time to make these moccasins," Matthew said. No, Maria told him, it only took a few hours to bead a pair of moccasins. She's been doing beadwork all her life.

Morningstar ordered moccasins for herself and Matthew. Maria said they'd be ready the next day.

Next Morningstar wanted Matthew to meet her cousin, John Piche. John is Cree and lives on the Mikisew Cree Reservation, near Fort Chipewyan. He is a traditional hunter and trapper. He works as a tour guide, bringing tourists to the woods and lake to camp or fish. John does not like to kill animals for sport, so he doesn't take sport hunters on tours. He believes it is important to respect animals and the environment. He kills only for food.

John took Morningstar and Matthew for a boat ride along the river. Matthew sat in the front of the boat so he could have a good view. John steered the boat, watching for tree stumps sticking out of the water. They stopped at one of John's favorite places along the river, and Matthew helped carry the gear ashore.

Matthew tried his luck at fishing. Although the fish weren't biting, he enjoyed it.

*John Piche*

*John and Matthew mix dough for bannock.*

Matthew's mom told him to come and watch John make bannock. Bannock is considered a traditional bread for Native people—even though the tradition only goes as far back as the fur trading days. Matthew had watched his mom bake bannock in an oven, but he had never seen it cooked outdoors.

John mixed flour, salt, baking powder, lard, and water into a dough. Matthew made some dough, too. But he put in too much water, and the dough got sticky. He had to add more flour. After Matthew and John finished mixing and kneading the dough, John fried it in a pan over the fire. It took about 20 minutes to cook.

After the bannock was done, John fried some moose meat. He had killed the moose himself. Matthew thought the moose meat tasted great. He wished he could have it more often, but grocery stores in the city don't sell moose meat.

After the three of them had eaten, they walked in the woods. An eagle flew nearby. "It came to bless us," Matthew's mom said.

John showed Matthew some herbs and roots, such as muskeg and spruce gum, that Indian people pick and use for medicinal purposes. Muskeg is in bogs. It's plant matter that looks and feels like soft, wet earth. Native people brew muskeg into a tea that helps people feel better when they're sick.

*Muskeg* (top left) *and spruce gum* (below left)

Hundreds of different plants, herbs, and roots can be used for medicine and food. Many Native people and others who live close to the land know how to use these plants. An elder named Snowbird taught John how to use plants and herbs for healing.

Later, when Matthew and his mom got back to town, they walked to the Lodge, the finest hotel in Fort Chipewyan. From the patio they could see most of the nearby islands. They watched the sun set before going home.

The next morning, Matthew wanted to sleep in, but he had to wake up early, at seven o'clock, because Joe Adam was going to take him and his mother out to set a fishing net.

Joe, a Chipewyan, is a friend of Morningstar. He is a fisherman, trapper, and hunter. Matthew and his mom met Joe at the dock. Before heading out on the lake, they put on life jackets. Matthew was still tired, but the cool wind blowing on his face soon woke him up. There was just enough wind on the lake to make the ride bumpy.

They rode for about 20 minutes before they reached the place where Joe wanted to set the fishing net. He slowed the boat down and turned off the motor before throwing the anchor overboard. Joe was sure he could catch some lake trout in this spot.

He looked at the clouds. "The wind will pick up from the southeast later in the day," he said. He could tell by the way the clouds were shaped. Joe has lived most of his life close to the land—not in a city. He knows how to watch the clouds and listen to the wind to tell what the weather will be.

Joe carefully untangled his fishing net before setting it into the water. The net was big, about 25 feet long. After the net was untangled, Joe threw a buoy into the water. Two buoys keep the net from sinking and mark its place so the fisherman can find it again.

As Joe set the net, he teased Matthew and his mom about living in the city too long.

"You should learn how to live off the land, the way your people have for hundreds of years, instead of buying everything from stores," he said. He laughed and told Matthew he couldn't survive on the land if he had to.

Matthew thought it was a good start to learn how to set a fishing net.

After the net was in the water, Joe tossed the other buoy into the water. "We'll come back tomorrow and pull the net in," he said.

Chipewyan Indians in Canada have the right to fish the waters of Lake Athabasca because of a treaty. When the European settlers came to North America, the original peoples had already been living there for thousands of years. As more and more settlers arrived, they took over the land where the Native people lived. The governments of Canada and the United States made treaties with the original people to help make up for the land that was being taken.

Many treaties gave Indians the right to continue traditional activities such as fishing and hunting. Some treaties gave Indian people areas of land called reservations or reserves. These areas were much, much smaller than the territory where the people had lived before. Many Native people were forced to move to reservations and not allowed to leave.

In 1899, the Chipewyan Indians and the Canadian government signed Treaty Number 8. Treaty 8 affects people living in a large area in Canada—most of northern Alberta, northeast British Columbia, the northwest corner of Saskatchewan, and the southern part of the Northwest Territories. In addition to reservation land, the treaty gives the Chipewyans hunting and fishing rights. Matthew's great-great-great-grandfather, Chief Laviolette, was one of the people who signed Treaty 8.

Every year the people of Fort Chipewyan have a celebration, called Treaty Days, in honor of the signing of Treaty 8. During Treaty Days, everyone gets together for games, dances, a talent show, and sports.

As Joe brought in the boat and docked it, Matthew could see people preparing for Treaty Days in town. Teepees were being set up and tables arranged for a feast.

Matthew had to get up early again the next day. He couldn't believe he'd only been here two days. The time had flown by. At home, Matthew stays busy with school and sports, especially track and field. He collects comic books, coins, and baseball cards. He also enjoys acting. He was in a television special called "Moccasin Flats."

Matthew wished he could play his Sega Game Gear for a while, but it was time to go out on the lake again with Joe. This time Joe brought his nephew, Donovan, and his grandson, Adam, along for a ride. The wind was stronger and colder today.

When they got to the place where they'd set the net, Joe threw the anchor in the water. He put on gloves to pull in the cold, slippery net. He showed Matthew how to bring in the net without tangling it. The boat rocked slowly back and forth as Joe pulled fish out of the net. There were 14, a good catch. Most of the fish were lake trout, along with some jack-fish. Joe placed the fish in a plastic box. Everyone sat quietly so they would not disturb Joe.

As they headed back to town, they could see the islands in the area. Fort Chipewyan is alive with activity during the summer. Many people come to fish, camp, and hunt.

In town, they went to Joe's house. He wanted to show Matthew how to smoke and dry fish. First he invited them in for some tea. After they drank the tea, they went out back to Joe's smoke hut, a small structure made of wood. In the old days, Chipewyans made smoke huts from the branches of pine trees. Joe's hut is made from plywood. A fire is built in the center of the hut, and the fish are hung above the fire, where they dry in the smoke.

Joe sharpened his knives for cutting the fish, and Matthew laid some grass on a table. The grass helps keep the table clean, since scaling, cutting, and cleaning fish is a messy job. Joe's grandson brought out a basin of water to use for cleaning the fish. Joe slid his knife along the fish to remove the scales.

Joe showed Matthew how to hold the fish and the knife. Then he let Matthew try scaling some fish. The fish were very slippery and hard to handle.

After the fish were scaled, Joe cut them open from the head down. One fish had eggs inside, which Joe removed. Fish eggs are considered a delicacy.

Matthew tried cutting the fish the way Joe did. It felt slimy. It was hard to cut the meat away from the bones. Matthew felt frustrated.

"You're doing a good job, Matthew," Joe said with a smile.

After they cut the fish, they sliced the meat into thin strips. Joe also fileted some of the fish. Fish filets have all the skin and bone removed. They can be baked or fried.

Cutting fish is easy for Joe, because he's been doing it for years. Once he even won a contest for making dried fish. The contest was based on speed and cutting the fish without wasting any of the meat.

Joe washed the fish strips in the basin of water. Then he hung them outside so the water could drip off. (The dripping water might put out the fire in the smoke hut.)

*Before being smoked, cut fish are washed and allowed to dry outside.*

As the washed fish dried, Joe built a fire in the smoke hut. Then he and Matthew hung the fish. They would be left to dry and smoke for a couple of days. Joe would keep the fire burning in the hut.

Dried fish is easy to pack and store. It is nutritious and tastes great. Some people like dipping it in melted butter and eating it with bannock.

After hanging the fish, Joe invited everyone in for fried fish with potatoes and tea.

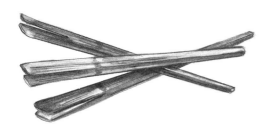

*T*he next day was the start of Treaty Days. It's a time for Indian people in Fort Chipewyan to gather and have a good time. The celebration lasts for two days. This year it was held at the high school.

Matthew watched people play traditional hand games. One team of players held bones and sticks in their hands, and another team had to guess who was hiding the bones or sticks. Matthew joined in the game. He had to be very alert and fast to guess who had the sticks. It was a lot of fun.

In the afternoon, the whole community gathered to share a traditional meal. Many people prepared food for the feast. There was moose meat, fish, bannock, soup, and other dishes. The elders were served first, to show respect for them. Then everyone else ate.

After the feast, there was a giveaway for the elders. A giveaway pays tribute to one or more people. Many gifts are given away in honor of that person. At this giveaway, the younger people gave tobacco and blankets to the elders. In many Native cultures, tobacco is considered sacred. It might be smoked in a pipe or burned as an offering to the Creator. While the gifts were being given away, people told stories and jokes.

    As the sun set, everyone got ready for the drum dance. During a drum dance, people gather around a fire and drummers sing and drum and dance late into the evening.

    The drummers warmed up by the fire. They sang a prayer song before they danced. The prayer song thanked the Creator for life, good health, and good spirits.

    The dance began. It lasted well into the evening. Matthew started to feel tired, but he kept dancing. Dancing kept the mosquitoes away and kept him warm.

Long ago, drum dances sometimes lasted for days. The original people of Fort Chipewyan traveled in small groups by dogsled during the winter and by canoe or on foot in the summer. Whenever groups gathered together, the beating of drums sounded. Drum dances were held around the fire, then as now. The dances were both a social event and a spiritual gathering at which the sacred pipe was passed.

As the people danced late into the night, they could see the Northern Lights in the sky. The Chipewyans believe that the lights are the ancestors dancing with them. The lights move and shake like dancers.

In the past, Métis people also held many gatherings at Fort Chipewyan every year. Fiddlers played music and people danced the jig and square dances. Even now there are a few good Métis fiddlers. Matthew's late great-grandfather, Emile Mercredi, was a fiddler. So is Matthew's grandfather, John Mercredi.

That night Matthew went to bed exhausted, but his mind was filled with the sound of drumming and singing. The next day would be his last full day in Fort Chipewyan. Everything was moving so fast! It was hard to believe the trip was almost over.

The first thing he and his mom did in the morning was to pick up their moccasins from Maria Houle. They were beautiful. Matthew tried his on, and they fit just right. Now he had moccasins to dance in that night. He thanked Maria before he and his mom went back to Treaty Days.

*Matthew and his mom get ready for the second day of Treaty Days.*

Matthew was happy to see that there were track and field races for kids and adults. He won two sprint races. He watched his mother race, too. The second day of the celebration passed as quickly as the first had, full of good food and drumming and dancing.

*Matthew inspects the dried fish. He can't wait to taste it!*

Finally it was time to leave. Before Matthew and Morningstar caught the plane, they went to pick up their dried fish. It looked delicious. Matthew was proud he had made it. He packed the fish in a bag to take home to relatives in the south.

There wasn't much time left to say goodbye and thank you to everyone. Matthew was sad. He wished they could stay longer, but he knew they had to leave. The vacation was over, and it was time for his mom to go back to work in Edmonton. He would come back to visit again, though. He was surprised at how much he had learned about his Chipewyan, Cree, and Métis heritage. Matthew told his mom he had a lot to be proud of. Maybe the next time he came, he would go moose hunting with John Piche.

# Word List

**bannock**—a light, fluffy bread that is baked or fried

**Chipewyan**—one of the original peoples of northwestern Canada; they call themselves *Denedeh* or *Dené*

**Cree**—one of the original peoples of Canada

**elders**—older people who are respected and admired for their knowledge and experience

**giveaway**—giving presents in honor of one or several people

**Métis**—people whose parents or ancestors are a mixture of European and Indian, such as French and Cree

**muskeg**—a bog, or a deposit of soft vegetative matter

**reserve**—an area of land that Indian people kept through agreement with the government of Canada or the United States; also called reservation

**treaty**—an agreement or arrangement made between two or more groups or governments, often with a signed contract

# *For Further Reading*

Dickason, Olive Patricia. *Canada's First Nations: A History of Founding Peoples from Earliest Times.* Toronto: McClelland & Stewart, 1992.

Dramer, Kim. *The Chipewyan.* Indians of North America. Frank W. Porter III, gen. ed. New York: Chelsea House, 1996.

Symington, Fraser. *The First Canadians.* Toronto: Natural Science of Canada Ltd., 1978.

Yates, Sarah. *Alberta.* Minneapolis: Lerner Publications Company, 1995.

### We Are Still Here
### Native Americans Today

48